NOT-FOR-PARENTS

THIS IS NOT A GUIDEBOOK. And it's definitely not for parents. It is the real inside story about one of the world's most famous cities – New York. In this book you'll hear fascinating tales about towering **skyscrapers** and deep subways, a **naked cowboy** and the **Yankees** loudest fans.

Check out cool stories about hot dogs and **snapping alligators**, bulls in the stock exchange and sports on the street. You'll find superheroes, famous battles, **cops**, cooks and **millions of rats**.

This book shows you a **NEW YORK** your parents probably don't even know about.

WHY THE BIG APPLE?

Horses love apples. So? Stable hands, trainers and jockeys used to call horse races in New York the big apples, meaning the biggest prize a horse could win. Turf racing writer John J. FitzGerald decided to call his weekly column for the *New York Morning Telegraph* 'Notes from around the Big Apple'. The name stuck!

KUDOS CORNER

In honour of John FitzGerald – Jack to his friends – a corner near his home was given the name 'Big Apple Corner'.

Food for thought
The apple is the official New York state fruit, and the apple muffin is the official state muffin. Who knew you could have an official state muffin?

GET KING KONG, HE'LL GRAPPLE WITH THAT APPLE!

W 54 ST

BIG APPLE CORNER

SENOR WENCES WAY

JOHN J. FITZGERALD

We can thank racing writer John J. FitzGerald for New York's nickname (he's the one holding the horse). In 1971, New York City began using the 'Big Apple' in tourist advertising. It was a bright, cheery image for a city that some people thought was dark and dangerous.

Dance the 'Big Apple'

Jazz musicians in the 1930s called paying gigs 'apples'. To get a paying gig in New York was the best of the best. There was a Big Apple jazz club and even a Big Apple dance craze.

Tales from the tracks

Eighty years ago New York was heavily into horse-racing. The competition was fierce, the stakes were high and sabotage was rife. Race-goers relied on reporters for honest information and many people caught on to the name Big Apple.

GOTHAM CITY

No, New York is not nicknamed Gotham because of Gotham City in Batman. Gotham is a small town in England whose folk, in the Middle Ages all pretended to be insane so that the tax collectors would stay away. Writer Washington Irving in the early 19th century used the name when talking about the people of New York City. Later, when Bob Kane and Bill Finger created Batman, the name Gotham suited a city riddled with bizarre criminals!

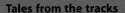

WANT MORE?

PACK YOUR TRUNKS

If you were on holiday in New York in the late 1800s, you could stay in an elephant. Hotel that is. The hotel was built when Coney Island – not really an island but a peninsula with a long beach – was the summer playground for New Yorkers.

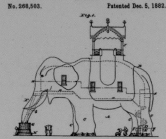

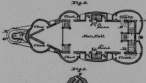

(No Model.)

J. V. LAFFERTY.
BUILDING.

No. 268,503.   Patented Dec. 5, 1882.

Colossal accommodation
The Elephant Hotel, also known as the Elephantine Colossus, was made of wood and tin. It was six storeys high with the guest rooms inside the main body of the elephant.

I'M THE WEINER!

HOT CONTEST

Every 4 July there is a hot dog eating contest held at Nathan's Famous hot dog stand which opened on Coney Island in 1916. The record is 68 hot dogs in 10 minutes. Could you beat that?

HARD TIMES

Back when it was buzzing, Coney Island had three amusement parks with state-of-the-art rides, including the Cyclone roller coaster which is a National Historic Landmark. But fires like the one that burned down the Elephant Hotel regularly wreaked havoc. Then the Great Depression hit in the 1930s and no-one could afford much amusement...

Coney cool

These days Coney Island is considered cool because of its very long beach and the walkway that runs alongside it, the aquarium – which is the only one in New York City – and the new Luna Park.

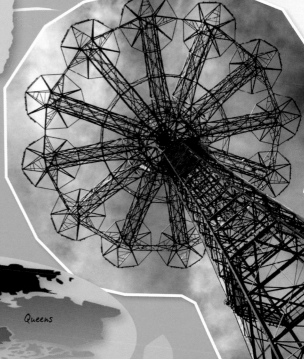

Manhattan

Queens

Brooklyn

Staten island

Coney Island is a peninsula!

WANT MORE?

Coney Island ☆ www.coneyisland.com

New Angoulême

Manna Hata

New Amsterdam

Henry Hudson sails up a river past an island the Indians call Manna Hata. After Henry, the river becomes known as Hudson River.

The people of the Netherlands, known as the Dutch, take over the island and rename Manna Hata New Amsterdam after their capital city back home.

1524

1609

1624

Giovanni da Verrazzano, in command of the French ship *La Dauphine*, sails into Upper New York Bay. He names the area New Angoulême, says hello to the locals, and heads off on the rest of his voyage.

First locals
The first New Yorkers were the Lenape tribes who arrived in the neighbourhood about 9000 years before the Dutch.

WHOSE NEW YORK?

Had things gone differently, New Yorkers could be saying 'een goede dag verder' instead of 'have a nice day'. The Dutch were the first white settlers in the area, but they were overtaken by the British which is why English is spoken in America. Of course it's far from being the only language. People from all over the world have made the city home and brought their native language with them. There could be as many as 800 languages spoken in New York!

New York

United States of America

Manhattan, Brooklyn, Bronx, Queens and Staten Island

1664

The English took New Amsterdam off the Dutch without too much of an argument. They rename the town New York in honour of the Duke of York who is the brother of the English king.

Americans want to get rid of the English and run their country themselves. There's a war, called the Revolutionary War and the Americans win. The new country is named the United States of America.

1775

1783

The modern City of New York is formed from five areas called boroughs: Manhattan, Brooklyn, Bronx, Queens and Staten Island.

1898

What's in a name?
'Ownership' of New York over time by different groups of people is remembered in place names: the Lenape name Manna Hata became Manhattan while the Dutch name Greenwijck became Greenwich Village.

HISTORY SURVIVES

Manhattan's oldest building, Fraunces Tavern, was built in 1719 as a private home. In 1763 it became a tavern and has been serving food and drink ever since.

IT'S MINE!

IT'S MINE!

IT'S MINE!

WANT MORE?

In 1626, the Dutch bought Manhattan Island for 60 guilders or $24!

GROUND ZERO

On September 11 in 2001 two passenger jets were flown into the twin towers of the World Trade Center in New York as an act of warfare. Thousands of people were killed, including many involved in the rescue efforts. On the tenth anniversary of the attacks an on-site memorial was opened to the public.

Day of horror
The day the two hijacked planes crashed into the Twin Towers in Manhattan, two other planes were also hijacked. One was flown into the Pentagon – the headquarters of the US Department of Defense in Washington DC. The fourth plane crashed into a field.

Wounded city
The void left by the demolition and removal of the Twin Towers was given the name 'Ground Zero' which means the point on the ground where a bomb has gone off.

SIGNS OF PEACE

As a way of expressing their grief and their sympathy, ceramic artists from around the world took part in a project called 'Tiles for America', creating special tiles that reflected on the tragedy. All sorts of tributes were left at makeshift memorials.

IN MEMORY

A memorial – officially called the National September 11 Memorial – includes almost 400 trees planted around two huge pools filled by massive waterfalls, each taking up the footprint of the Twin Towers. Etched in bronze around the waterfalls are the names of the 2979 people who died in the September 11 attacks and in the bombing of New York's World Trade Center in 1993.

Rising from the ashes

Beside the memorial a new tower is rising. When completed, One World Trade Center will be the tallest building in the United States at 541m (1776ft).

WANT MORE?

The 9/11 Memorial – www.national911memorial.org

TYPICAL FOOD? Hmmm...

In a city founded by Dutch people that became home to freed African slaves, Jewish people escaping horror at home, Chinese looking for gold, Irish in search of a job, and millions of others from all parts of the world, it's hard to say what the typical food of New York City is!

Washington Heights: Dominican, Puerto Rican and Jewish

Harlem: African-American, Latin American and West Indian

East Harlem: Puerto Rican, Mexican, Dominican

Upper West Side: German, Thai, Modern American

East Village: Japanese, Korean, Indian and Ukranian

Little Italy: Italian and Chinese

Lower East Side: Puerto Rican, Kosher and Latin American

Chinatown: Chinese

HEAD FOR BREAD

The Big Apple is the *bagel* and *bialy* capital of America. Every New Yorker has a favourite place to buy them and way to eat them. A *bagel* is a simple, doughnut-shaped bread that is boiled and then baked. A *bialy* (say 'bee-AH-lee') is a chewy roll with onions baked into a dent in the centre.

Food stamps
Migrants have made their mark on areas of the city with the foods and eating habits of their homelands. It all changes as they move on and others take their place, like Little Italy which is much more Asian now.

Hard to choose
'Deli' in New York is a style of food that includes overstuffed sandwiches served with pickles and a 'wet' salad such as coleslaw or potato salad.

IN A PICKLE

People in New York are passionate about pickles. Cured cucumbers have been a staple food from the time of the first immigrants because they keep well. Different pickle producers have their own mix of spices, including mustard seed, bay leaves, peppercorns and garlic. Once a New Yorker picks a pickle as a favourite, they stay loyal!

Can you match the food in the picture to the foods listed?

Slice of New York

New Yorkers never ask for a piece of pizza – it's always a 'slice' and they don't even bother with 'of pizza'. A plain slice means a piece of cheese pizza. A 'pie' is a whole pizza.

1. bagel
2. dumplings
3. pierogis
4. pastrami on rye
5. pickles
6. pizza
7. black and white cookie

WANT MORE?

Get in a pickle! – www.howtopickle.com

BATTLE OF BROOKLYN

England had ruled the American colonies for around 175 years when they decided they wanted to run themselves. The English weren't thrilled, so war was declared. The first battle was fought in Brooklyn in New York, where American commander-in-chief, George Washington, had set up his troops. The English army and navy slam-dunked the Americans in that battle but Washington went on to win the war – which is why Americans don't have a English accent.

Musket

Tin canteen with wooden plug

Garters

Hand-sewn boots – no left or right!

Typical soldier

Battle fashio
The soldiers from Delaware had nice blue jackets with red facings and white waistcoats. These later became the uniform for the Continental Army formed to represent the whole country in the fight for independence.

REMIND ME AGAIN HOW I GET STUCK ON THE FRONT LINE?!

FACE-OFF

The boss of America in 1776 was King George III of England. Instead of protecting America and helping it to grow, he squeezed the Americans for money and forced them to buy English products. As a landowner, George Washington directly experienced the squeeze. In his role as commander-in-chief of the American army he passionately faced off against King George – and went on to become the first American president!

Washington

King George III

THE SIX-YEAR WAR OF INDEPENDENCE

YIKES! LET'S GET OUTTA HERE!

Politics and principles

Washington became a soldier at the age of 22, fighting for the British against the French. After inheriting a huge amount of land he left the army and went into politics. Ten years later, as things hotted up in the conflict between America and England, he joined the army again – and the rest is history!

British flag
1606–1801

American flag
1775–77

What went down in Brooklyn

When Washington was made chief of the Continental Army he headed for Brooklyn. With 20,000 soldiers Washington thought he was ready to rock-n'-roll. Unfortunately he was outnumbered and outsmarted by the British, who surrounded him. He was forced to retreat.

WANT MORE?

Battle of Brooklyn – www.brooklynonline.com/history/battle

SWAMP CENTRAL TO CENTRAL PARK

In the mid-19th century, immigrants were pouring into New York and the place was getting mighty crowded. People were crying out for a place where they could get some peace and quiet. Eventually a plan was hatched to create a park out of a stretch of boggy swamps and rocky outcrops. The result: Central Park – twice the size of the world's smallest country!

From bog to beautiful
In 1857 work began on a park design called the Greensward Plan. It took 15 years to turn swampland into wonderland.

Making way for the park
Not all of the land used for the park was swamp. In some areas houses, churches, shops and schools were torn down along with shanty towns where poor people lived illegally.

Animal attractions

The original design didn't include a zoo, but park staff started looking after stray animals, and a zoo was eventually built. It now houses polar bears, pandas, snakes and sea lions!

Green scene

Central Park is now the back yard for over 1.6 million people who live in Manhattan. With baseball fields and tennis courts, 20 different playgrounds, boating on the lake, a carousel, a castle and a swimming pool that becomes an ice-skating rink in winter, Central Park is the kind of back yard we all wish we had!

WANT MORE?

In the mid-1800s, group picnics were banned in the park. ☆ www.centralpark.com

All the rage
New York designer James Wilson put together this fashion line-up for the winter of 1835–36. The hand-coloured print was part of a new era in advertising, pushing a link between fashion and social advantage.

I THINK MY HAIR IS FLAMMABLE

IT'S IN FASHION

The invention of the sewing machine sent New York into overdrive. Suddenly clothes could be made fast and in bulk. Slavemasters in America's south spent loads of money in New York buying off-the-rack clothing for slaves. Then immigrants from Europe with expert sewing skills flooded into the city, and it became possible to make beautiful copies of top French designs. Local designers got in on the act and the Garment District of New York became fashion central.

It's a tough job...
The behind-the-scenes reality of New York's clothing industry is a long way from long-legged models on catwalks and funky window displays...

Seventh Ave
439 - 421
Fashion Ave

Vintage threads in Nolita

FIT FOR FASHION

Where there's a clothing industry there's a mannequin manufacturing industry too. Mannequins – also called dummies – are used to display clothing in stores. Thousands of mannequins are made in New York. There are also plenty of live mannequins, called 'fit models'. Because they can walk and talk, fit models help designers and manufacturers to know if a zipper is uncomfortable, if the fabric is itchy and whether a dress will stay in place when it's on a real person!

Seventh Avenue boutiques

FASHION FAVOURITES

Clothes manufacturing is mostly now done overseas, but the Big Apple is still the hot spot for new American fashion. Top designers like Vera Wang, Donna Karan and Calvin Klein have their bases in New York. The Garment District is also a hub for fabulous fabrics and all the bits that go with sewing, like threads, buttons and trims.

WANT MORE?

The Fashion Center – www.fashioncenter.com

BEST VIEW

The Empire State Building was the tallest building in the world for forty years and has been the tallest building in New York twice. The first time was from its completion in 1931 until 1972, when the World Trade Center was built. It regained its title in the worst sort of way when the World Trade Center was destroyed in 2001.

Up in lights

A great hairy ape has climbed the building twice. First in the 1933 film *King Kong*, and again in a 2005 remake. Kong falls to his death in both films after being attacked by airplanes.

ON THE WAY UP

The One World Trade Center, also known as Freedom Tower, is under construction. When it's finished it will be 541m (1776ft) high, making it the tallest building in the United States.

Empire State: 381m (1250ft)

former Twin Towers: 417m (1368ft)

ART DECO

The Empire State Building was built in the 1930s when the 'Art Deco' style reigned supreme. This style was influenced by technology, fashion, jazz music and even ancient Egyptian art.

103 Number of storeys in the building – plus there's a 62m (203ft) tower on top.

6514 That's how many windows there are in the Empire State – imagine having to clean all those!

73 The number of lifts in the building – better options than climbing 1872 steps!

40 The number of years the Empire State was the world's tallest building.

Seemed like a good idea at the time...
The building's spire was designed as a dock for giant airships. This only happened once, and that didn't work so well, so it was never tried again.

ONLY 6,513 TO GO!

High and mighty
About four million people a year travel up to the observatories on the 86th and 102nd floors to enjoy 360-degree views of Manhattan and beyond.

WANT MORE?

Lightning strikes the building about 100 times a year. ☆ www.esbnyc.com

BRIGHT IDEA

Anyone who owns a building in Times Square is required by law to attach an illuminated sign to the outside. This means that neon lights, big screens, flashing logos and endlessly running 'news ticker' displays are part of Times Square's special appeal.

TOURIST TIMES 2000

If you don't like crowds, stay away from Times Square. It's the number one tourist spot in the United States – 2000 people pass through it every 15 minutes! They call this massive intersection of Broadway and Seventh Avenue 'The Crossroads of the World' – it's filled with people from everywhere.

Naked ambition
This Times Square regular is Robert Burck, known as the Naked Cowboy. He's not really nude… he wears a cowboy hat, boots, underpants and a guitar!

Play Times
The Toys 'R' Us store in Times Square is the world's largest toy store. It even has its own indoor Ferris Wheel!

New Times Ahead!
New Year's Eve was first celebrated in Times Square in 1904. With its famous ball-lowering ceremony, it's now a massive event every year.

Melting moments
One of Times Square's biggest attractions is Madame Tussauds Wax Museum, with more than 200 life-like figures of celebrities, sports stars, and people from history.

WANT MORE?

Times Square – www.timessquarenyc.org

Bats in the Big Apple
Six species of bats hang
around in New York's Central
Park, though sadly a disease
called White Nose Syndrome is
killing many of the bats in the
New York area. Bats are sometimes
called flying mice, but they're not
closely related.

IT'S A JUNGLE OUT THERE

It's impossible to count how many cats and dogs there
are in New York – three million is a guesstimate. And
with so many people living in apartments, household
pets spend most of their time indoors. But in the
streets and parks of the city, there are plenty of
animals on the loose. From squirrels, skunks and
seals to beavers, bats and bald eagles, New York
really is a concrete jungle.

JUST-IN BEAVER

New York has always been big on
beavers. Once upon a time warm,
waterproof beaver fur protected
local Indians from the cold, and made
a lot of money for traders when beaver
hats became all the rage in Europe. But
the beavers were eventually hunted out,
and for 200 years not one beaver was seen
near New York. Then Jose appeared in the
Bronx River! He instantly became a celebrity,
and has now been joined by a friend, named –
you guessed it – Justin!

Muskrat

Confident coyotes

The city's not the safest spot for a wild dog, but over the years some adventurous coyotes have ended up on the streets of Manhattan and in Central Park, probably by following train tracks, river banks and linked parks from suburban and country areas.

RAT CITY

It was once thought that New York rats lived mostly in the city's subways, dining on tossed takeaway. Now it's said that the rat population is out of control, and that for every person in New York there's at least one rat! The government has even set up a hotline for rat sightings!

Deer here

The deer of New York that disappeared 200 years ago when forests were chopped down for firewood now seem to be returning to the parks of New York City!

OH RATS, HAS ANYONE SEEN MY KEYS?

how many babies can a mama rat have in a year?

285

Keeping company

Before Justin arrived to keep Jose company, Jose hung out with a muskrat called Sebastian.

Beaver

WANT MORE?

SESAME STREET

Everyone knows about this famous imaginary street on the West Side of Manhattan. The *Sesame Street* TV series has proven so popular since it started more than 40 years ago that there's even a Sesame Street Day held in New York on November 10. Fans of the show visit Amsterdam Avenue to see houses that inspired the show's buildings.

The man behind the Muppets
The puppeteer Jim Henson created the original *Sesame Street* Muppets including Kermit the Frog.

Furry and famous
Plenty of real people have appeared on *Sesame Street*, but the real stars are the Muppets like Bert and Ernie, Big Bird, Elmo, Grover and Cookie Monster.

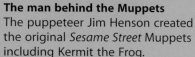

GROVER GOES GLOBAL

Sesame Street is the most widely watched children's television show in the world! It's broadcast in more than 100 countries and there are a bunch of versions adapted for local children. Big Bird is Big Business!

Match the names to the countries

1. *Sesame Tree*   a. India

2. *Vila Sésamo*   b. Tanzania

3. *Jalan Sesama*   c. Brazil

4. *Galli Galli Sim Sim*   d. Indonesia

5. *Rue Sésame*   e. Poland

6. *El Mundo de Elmo*   f. Northern Ireland

7. *Sezamkowy Zakątek*   g. France

8. *Kilimani Sesame*   h. Mexico

I AM A REAL TV STAR!

Answers: 1–f, 2–c, 3–d, 4–a, 5–g, 6–h, 7–e, 8–b

Celebrity street
The show has had hundreds of famous special guests, including the US president's wife, Michelle Obama, the Harlem Globetrotters basketball team, actor Natalie Portman and singer will.i.am.

Humble beginnings
When *Sesame Street* began in 1969, the street was pretty rundown. And there were only four cast members: Bob, Gordon, Susan and Mr Hooper – along with real New York children.

WANT MORE?

The same actor has played Big Bird since 1969 ☆ www.sesamestreet.org

NEW YORK'S FINEST

Back in the day, New York police went around on horseback and shook a wooden rattle to warn of danger. Now with eight million people to look after, a wooden rattle just doesn't make the grade and it takes more than a horse to enforce the law in the Big Apple.

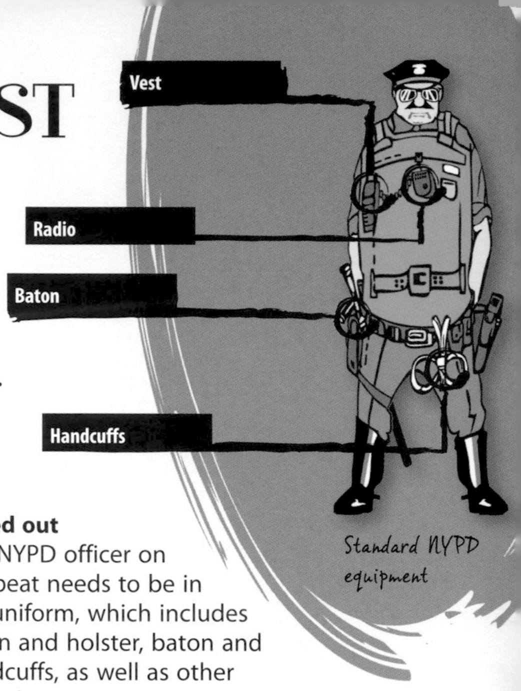

Vest

Radio

Baton

Handcuffs

Standard NYPD equipment

A moving story
New York police use all kinds of vehicles in their work; a whole variety of cars, buses and four-wheel drives to bicycles, scooters, motorcycles, horses and helicopters. They even ride beach buggies on Coney Island!

Kitted out
The NYPD officer on the beat needs to be in full uniform, which includes a gun and holster, baton and handcuffs, as well as other special equipment.

POLICE

POLICE

POLICE

NYPD

Top cops

The NYPD has ten separate bureaus, each one with a chief who reports to the Police Commissioner. There are also some specialised units, including a Movie and Television Unit to help people filming in the city.

BRING IT, BADDIES!

POLICE DIV.2

PATCH IT UP

The NYPD badge, or patch, has been in use for 40 years. It features the scales of justice, an English sailor and a native American. Then there's an eagle in the middle, which represents the US government.

ANIMALS IN BLUE

About 120 horses, 30 German Shepherds and 3 bloodhounds serve in the NYPD. The horses are trained to stay calm around noises such as sirens, noisy crowds and gunfire!

WANT MORE?

PLAY BALL

Classic Yankees cap

Loyal and lively or just rowdy and rude? The Bleacher Creatures are full-on fans of the New York Yankees baseball team, famous for their utter devotion to their team and nastiness to the fans of other teams. They rave, chant and sing at the games, starting with the 'Roll Call' – at the beginning of every game the Bleacher Creatures chant the name of each player until they get a response like a wave or a nod, or some special acknowledgement.

Countless and priceless
Yankees caps can be found in most parts the world – but the ball above is one of a kind because it was signed by the great Babe Ruth.

BILLION-DOLLAR BALLPARK

Yankee Stadium was opened in the Bronx in 2009 to replace, well, Yankee Stadium. It was built across the road from the old stadium that had been the Yankees' home ground since 1923. It is believed to be the third most expensive stadium ever built.

The bleachers

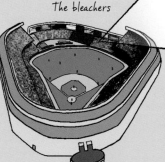

Bleach balls
The bleacher seats are high up over the outfield fences, so they are cheap – and from there fans sometimes catch balls hit for home runs.

1 CITY, 2 TEAMS

The New York Mets is the city's other big baseball team. It's based in the borough of Queens. They play each other at least once a season and it's always a full house at the stadium.

The sultan of swat
George 'Babe' Ruth was a seven-time World Series champion. Almost 100 years since he joined the Yankees, he's still their most famous player.

Mets home   away

Yankees home   away

WANT MORE?

The New York Yankees – www.yankees.com

MERCI!

This is one gift you would have trouble wrapping… The 93-metre (305ft) high Statue of Liberty was a gift from the French to the Americans to celebrate their independence from the English. Alexandre Eiffel who created the Eiffel Tower built the internal frame for the copper statue. She was sculpted by Frederic Bartholdi and put together on the site of an old fort, now called Liberty Island.

> THE REAL NAME OF THE STATUE IS 'LIBERTY ENLIGHTENING THE WORLD'.

GODDESS

The female figure in Roman robes is Libertas, the ancient goddess of freedom. The torch she holds represents enlightenment and keeping the flame of freedom alive.

The artist's inspiration
Images of Libertas and her utensils of freedom, like those found on ancient Roman coins, inspired the sculptor.

ARRIVÉE D'ÉMIGRANTS JUIFS A NEW-YORK

Top view
Her crown has seven spikes representing the seven continents and seven seas. Inside the crown is an observation deck. To get there you climb 354 narrow steps. Inside, the crown can be 10°C (20°F) hotter than outside!

Welcome to your new home
The statue faces southeast, greeting ships as they arrive into New York. She became a symbol of hope and freedom for immigrants coming to America to start a new life.

Liberty in pieces
She was shipped from France in 350 pieces and assembled over four months, opening in 1886. New Yorkers had already glimpsed the size of the gift they were to receive – the arm and torch had been on display in Madison Square Park for six years.

I JUST GET CARRIED AWAY SOMETIMES...

WANT MORE?

Lady Liberty's nose is 1.37m (4ft 6in) long! ☆ www.nps.gov/stli

CHINATOWN

GRRRR

A whole lot of people from China came to America in the 1850s to work in the goldfields of California or on the railroads being built across the country. When the gold ran out and the railroads were built many moved east to the big cities where they found employment in manufacturing, or started up small businesses like laundries. Living near each other protected them from racism, and created Chinatown!

Culture in Columbus
Columbus park in Chinatown is a neighbourhood hang and home turf for Chinese chess and checkers, mah jong, martial arts, tai chi and Chinese opera.

ON THE MOVE

Manhattan Chinatown is a place to live and a place to do business for many Chinese in New York. It's also a place where locals and tourists can eat well and score a bargain, but it's not the only Chinatown in the city. Growing communities of Chinese people in the boroughs of Queens and Brooklyn are creating other Chinatowns.

Choice from China
Manhattan's Chinatown has masses of markets, restaurants and food stalls offering various styles of cooking from different regions of China, from salty, noodle-based Mandarin cuisine to spicy, rice-based food from Szechuan.

With his huge mouth Nian ate many villagers in one gulp!

CHINESE NEW YEAR

The most important holiday for Chinese people the world over is Chinese New Year. A parade through the streets acts out the legend of a terrible monster named Nian – the Chinese word for year – who is frightened off with loud noises from drums and firecrackers as well as red paper cutouts on doors. Each year around 5000 people take part in the New York parade for Chinese New Year with fancy floats and acrobats, musicians, magicians and marching bands.

MMM... CHINESE FOOD...

WANT MORE?

Chinatown, Manhattan – www.explorechinatown.com

SECRETS OF GRAND CENTRAL

Manhattan's Grand Central Terminal, opened in 1913, is one of the world's busiest train stations. There's more to this station than meets the eyes of the 750,000 people who pass through it every day – hidden staircases, a secret sub-basement and the disused Track 61 under the fancy Hotel Waldorf-Astoria. Special guests like generals and presidents would arrive on Track 61 in private trains then take a lift from the platform up into the hotel.

For 20 years there was an art school in the attic of the station.

LOST AND FOUND

With millions of people passing through the station each year, there are bound to be a few odd items lost and found. As well as the usual lost and found phones, shoes, bags and books, there have been false teeth, a pair of earlobes left by a plastic surgeon and one very sad basset hound!

Soccer boots

Earlobes

Shopping bags

Mobile phones

False teeth

Lost dog!

Jewellery

Hey, have you heard of M42?

PSSST!

Can't miss it
It's no secret that the information booth in the main concourse has a four-faced clock. Being unmissable, it's often used as a meeting place.

Celestial ceiling
The star-studded gold leaf ceiling of Grand Central was painted by the French artist Paul Helleu in 1912. It used to have 10-watt bulbs which had to be replaced regularly. Now it has energy-efficient, longer-lasting fibre-optic lights.

Where they keep the electricity generators...

It's not on any maps of the station!

SSHHHH...
Those in the know call it 'the whispering gallery' – the area in front of the Oyster Bar restaurant where low arches carry sound so perfectly that a whisper can be heard clearly on the other side of the building. There's no sign marking it which makes it another of the great secrets of Grand Central Terminal.

WANT MORE?

Grand Central Terminal – www.grandcentralterminal.com

RIPPED OFF?

Back in 1626, a guy named Peter Minuit was put in charge of a tiny Dutch settlement named New Amsterdam. He was prepared to do whatever was necessary to take over from the Lenape Indians who'd lived there for around 10,000 years. He found them easygoing, so instead of killing them he bought Manhattan Island from them. He gave them goods worth 60 Dutch guilders – around $24 – and they gave him the Big Apple.

I'M TELLING YOU – CAPES ARE SO HOT RIGHT NOW

Living on the land
The Lenape called their territory Lenapehoking and their name for what is now Manhattan was Manna Hata. They lived by growing crops of corn, squash and beans, by hunting and fishing, and by gathering berries and nuts.

Happy families
The Lenape lived in either wigwams or longhouses that could accommodate a few families.

PEEKABOO

Young Lenape men pulled their hair out leaving a small crest on the head.

Trade off

White settlers traded heavily with local Indians for fur which could get a good price in Europe. In return, the Lenape were given manufactured goods like glass beads, mirrors, kettles, fishing hooks, iron axes and alcohol.

Sacred shell beads

Axe head

Drilling tool

Kettle

Mouth harp

HALL OF HISTORY

Over time the local Lenape Indians lost access to the resources they had lived on in the past. They also died from diseases brought over by white settlers. Some Lenape tribes survived and are now in Oklahoma and Kansas. The National Museum of American Indians in New York tells the story of the Lenape and other Native Americans.

Friendly folk

With an environment so rich in resources, the Lenape had no reason to be mean-spirited. They shared what they had with visitors, they didn't steal from each other, and they chose their chiefs for honesty, wisdom and spiritual understanding.

THE ART OF RESOURCEFULNESS

Using the resources of nature, such as stone and wood along with the bones, gut, muscle, hair and hide of animals, the Lenape crafted tools, clothing, utensils, weapons, furniture, transport, ceremonial masks and artwork.

WANT MORE?

The Lenape had three clans – Wolf, Turtle and Turkey. Each was led by a Clan Mother.

ACTION ON FILM

Many of the world's most famous superheroes and mighty monsters started their action-packed lives in New York's thriving comic book industry and even those that were born elsewhere, seem to like to visit the city either to fight evil or wreak havoc. What works in the comics is sure to end up on the screen and New York has served as the backdrop to many thrilling movies.

Batman

COMIC BOOK HEROES

American comic books originated in the early 1930s. In the days before television, colour movies or video games they were a major source of entertainment and New York was where it all happened. Many of the characters invented back then are still going strong.

The Caped Crusader
Superhero Batman doesn't have any superpowers. He relies on his strength, detective skills and gadgets to fight crime. His adventures take place in Gotham City which is fictional but bears a strong resemblance to New York where his creators Bob Cane and Bill Finger lived and worked.

Spiderman

Man for sticky situations
Peter Parker was a regular New York teenager until he was bitten by a radioactive spider which turned him into – you guessed it – Spiderman! Now he can cling to walls which is a handy skill in a high-rise city.

In the movie King Kong vs Godzilla (1962) King Kong is the victor.

Superman

The Man of Steel
Superman came to Earth from the planet Krypton as a baby. When he's not saving the world he is Clark Kent, reporter for the *Daily Planet* newspaper. New York stood-in for his hometown Metropolis in the first Superman movie released in 1978.

Great ape
King Kong thrilled the world when he first appeared on screen in 1933. Stolen from his island home, King Kong is taken to New York to be exhibited on stage. Then he escapes and famously climbs to the top of the Empire State Building

Godzilla

King Kong

Large lizard on the loose!
Godzilla is a prehistoric reptillian monster that has appeared in comic books, television series, video games and over 30 – mostly Japanese – movies. In the 1998 movie *Godzilla*, he goes on the rampage in New York.

WANT MORE?

Which Superhero are you? – www.thesuperheroquiz.com

HARLEM

America might not have won independence from England if it weren't for a really annoying sound. During a battle fought where Harlem is today, George Washington's army were retreating from a big English force. To insult Washington, the English played their horns as though they were on a fox hunt. Washington was so annoyed that he turned his soldiers back against the English and fought until they won! That was the Battle of Harlem and it's still a lively neighbourhood.

Chillin' in the hoopdee

THE FOX IS RUNNING!'

HOW DARE YOU!

Battle of Harlem
Dutch settlers were the first Europeans to move here. They named the area Harlem after Haarlem in the Netherlands. England took the place from the Dutch and then in the Battle of Harlem Americans took the country from the English, but Harlem kept its name.

Talent quest

From the 1930s the Apollo theatre in Harlem was the hip place for upcoming African-American jazz and blues singers, dancers and comedians. It was also the only theatre in the city to hire African–Americans in backstage positions. The Apollo is still going strong.

Globetrotters

The Harlem Globetrotters mix fantastic basketball with comedy to entertain crowds in exhibition games. The 'Harlem' part of their name isn't because they are from New York. They actually started in Chicago but at the time, Harlem was the hot spot for African–American culture.

BOOYA!

Harlem (the pink bits on the map) is at the north end of Manhattan.

Hudson River

Hamilton Heights

East Harlem

Central Park

East River

RAP & BALL

The world's largest streetball tournament, the Entertainers Basketball Classic, happens at Rucker Park in Harlem. It started years ago as a friendly tournament between rap groups. Now it's televised, professional athletes take part and celebrities are always in the bleachers.

WANT MORE?

World's largest panoramic image – www.harlem-13-gigapixels.com

CHECK-IN AT ELLIS

Almost half of America's population are descended from immigrants who arrived by ship and entered the country through the immigration centre at Ellis Island in New York. Fourteen-year-old Annie Moore from Ireland became famous when she was the first immigrant to be checked in at Ellis Island back in 1892. Being the first, Annie was given a $10 gold piece – about a thousand dollars in today's money!

The world comes to New York
As many as 800 languages are spoken in New York, more than in any other city in the world.

In
1892
the Ellis Island Immigration Station was officially opened and in its first year, it processed

450,000
immigrants.

THAT'S MY GREAT GREAT AUNT THRICE REMOVED!

I HOPE LIVING IN AMERICA IS BETTER THAN THAT SMELLY BOAT

Naming family

There is now a museum in the old immigration station complex. As well as photos and stories the museum houses the Wall of Honor, a list of over 700,000 names of people who came to America through Ellis Island.

PASSING THE TEST

Immigrants could spend up to five hours at Ellis Island being asked questions about their level of education, the kind of work they could do and how much money they had. If they were sick they were sent home or put in the island's hospital.

From Ellis to everywhere

It is estimated that 40 out of every 100 Americans have at least one ancestor who came through Ellis Island. Immigrants still pour into New York but now they tend arrive at one of the city's three international airports.

WANT MORE?

Ellis Island – www.history.com/topics/ellis-island

THE CORKSCREW

Solomon Guggenheim was an art collector with a lot of money. Frank Lloyd Wright was an architect with attitude. Together they created the Guggenheim Museum in New York. It took 16 years to build but neither Guggenheim nor Wright lived to see it finished – or to hear the criticism that it looked like a corkscrew!

Walking on air
The reinforced concrete ramps have no supports at all – only the walls hold them in place. Sunlight from the glass dome floods down to every level.

MAN WITH A MISSION

Wright was an adventurous architect who aimed to create a building that would make a dramatic statement next to its boxy neighbours. It took Wright 15 years and 700 sketches to design the museum.

Model building

If you can't visit the Guggenheim Museum in New York you can make one yourself at home! It's one of the few buildings to have been honoured with its own Lego set.

Take it from the top

Visitors take lifts to the top and then walk down the spiral ramp, stopping to look at the paintings on walls.

Hidden talent

Guggenheim's niece, Peggy, was also an art collector, and she recognised talent in the work of a young artist, Jackson Pollock, who was employed at her uncle's first museum as a carpenter. His work is now exhibited at the Guggenheim in New York.

WANT MORE?

Guggenheim Museum – www.guggenheim.org/new-york

BRIDGE ON THE BRINK

In the mid-19th century, more and more people needed to cross the East River from Brooklyn to Manhattan to go to work. Since the ferries often got stuck in the ice in winter or were stopped by bad weather a bridge made sense. The Brooklyn Bridge was the longest suspension bridge in the world when it opened in 1883 and it's been a special part of the New York skyline ever since.

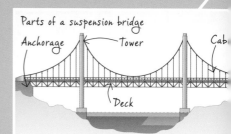

Parts of a suspension bridge

Anchorage · Tower · Cab

Deck

JUST WAVE AND LOOK HAPPY – JUST WAVE AND LOOK HAPPY...

The ultimate test
The first person to cross the bridge was the chief mechanic. He was pulled over on a main cable to show that it was safe.

Back to the future

The bridge is getting pretty old and so it is currently being rebuilt and repainted, which will take several years. Part of the challenge is working out how to redirect the 120,000 cars and 4000 pedestrians that cross the bridge every day.

All tucked in?

For workers building the bridge, there wasn't always time to go home at the end of a shift or even come down to ground level. So they slept in hammocks up in the cables instead! It was dangerous work. Many men fell to their deaths into the cold and turbulent East River.

A MOVING EXPERIENCE

Suspension bridges are designed to flex a little as they take the strain of moving traffic. But back in 1883 people expected their bridges to be rock-solid. A week after it opened, people walking the bridge panicked when they felt it moving, and there was a stampede in which 12 people were killed.

WANT MORE?

Brooklyn Bridge timeline – www.pbs.org/kenburns/brooklynbridge/timeline

THE BISON FROM THE BRONX!

Bronx Zoo started sending bison west to save them from extinction in 1907. They travelled by train to a nature reserve in Oklahoma in an attempt to rebuild a population that had been wiped out by hunting. Back then only about 1000 bison were left alive compared to between 30 and 60 million just a hundred years earlier. The plan worked, and now around 20,000 wild bison roam America's western plains.

Sanctuary in the city
The largest city zoo in the United States is located in parklands that were sold to New York City by a university for $1000.

Making a killing
The United States government supported the mass hunting of Bison herds back in the 19th century, and hunters made good money from selling skins as well as bones to make paint and glue.

GET EM' LEEROY!

FAT, FAST AND FURRY

Bison have been roaming the North American plains for thousands of years. Also known as American buffalo, they are the largest mammals in the United States. But even though they can weigh up to 1000kg (2200lb) each, they can still move quickly – up to 60km/h (37mph)!

LEAPING LEOPARDS

As well as boosting bison numbers, the Bronx Zoo plays an important role in the conservation of the endangered snow leopard. Careful! These leopards can leap – up to 14m (46ft) when they are ready for lunch.

Giving back the grasslands
The American Bison Society is working to restore almost half a million acres of wild-bison grazing lands across the United States, Canada and Mexico.

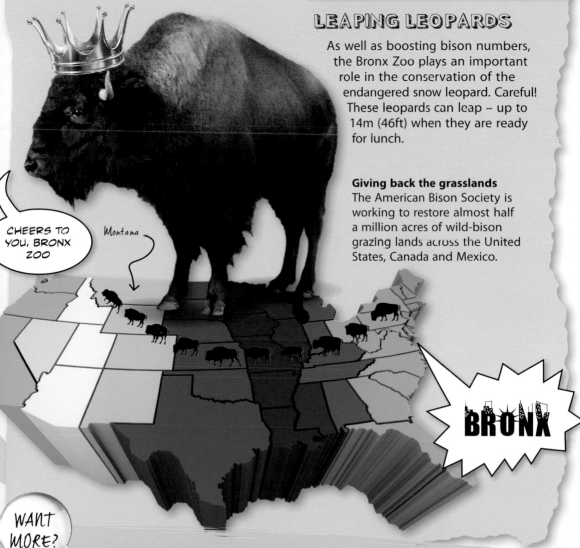

CHEERS TO YOU, BRONX ZOO

Montana

BRONX

WANT MORE?

Bronx Zoo – www.bronxzoo.com

THE DARING LADIES OF MoMA

The Museum of Modern Art (MoMA) in New York was considered outrageous when it opened. Three women, who became known as the 'daring ladies', rented a small space to use as an art gallery. Nothing new there. Only this gallery was different. The daring ladies only showed the latest art from Europe, and instead of a permanent collection, the art was shown for a while then moved on and new art brought in. What a concept!

Lillie P. Bliss

One of the founders of MoM. Bliss had an eye for art and owned works from the world best artists of the time. She left most of it to MoMA which was only two years old when she died.

YOU CALL THAT ART!?

The Starry Night by Vincent van Gogh

APPLAUSE PLEASE!

The museum, usually called MoMA, was the first gallery in the United States to only show modern art and to only have short exhibitions. Now it's one of the most important modern art museums in the world. If only the daring ladies were here to see it!

SO IT'S NEW, NO NEED TO HAVE AN ART ATTACK!

Abby Rockefeller

Rockefeller was a good friend of Lillie Bliss and was married to the son of the wealthiest man in the world! She liked works on paper and paid special attention to American art.

Mary Quinn Sullivan

Another founder of the museum, Mary Quinn was an art teacher married to an art collector, Cornelius Sullivan. She wanted as many people as possible to come to appreciate art at the museum.

Woman Writing by Pablo Picasso

Trafalgar Square by Mondrian

The Horse by Raymond Duchamp-Villon

Number 1 by Jackson Pollock

WANT MORE?

MoMA – www.moma.com

The Bronx

Manhattan

Queens

Brooklyn

Airport

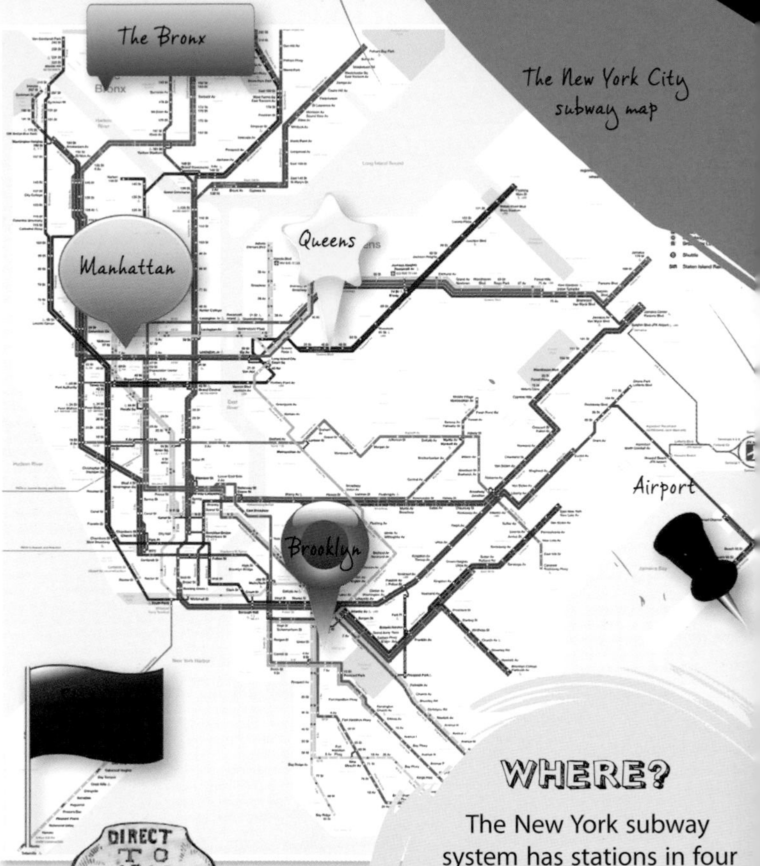

The New York City subway map

Streets ahead
New Yorkers were so relieved to have a subway system that when the first line opened in 1904, 150,000 people lined up to take the first ride. However, trolley cars continued to run on the streets until 1956.

OK, THAT'S LIKE THE FIFTH TIME. SOMEONE INVENT A SUBWAY!

DIRECT TO YORKVILLE & HARLEM

WHERE?
The New York subway system has stations in four of the city's five boroughs – Manhattan, Brooklyn, Queens and the Bronx. The fifth borough, Staten Island, is on the map but runs its own rail line. The subway system covers over 1300km (840 miles) not all of it underground.

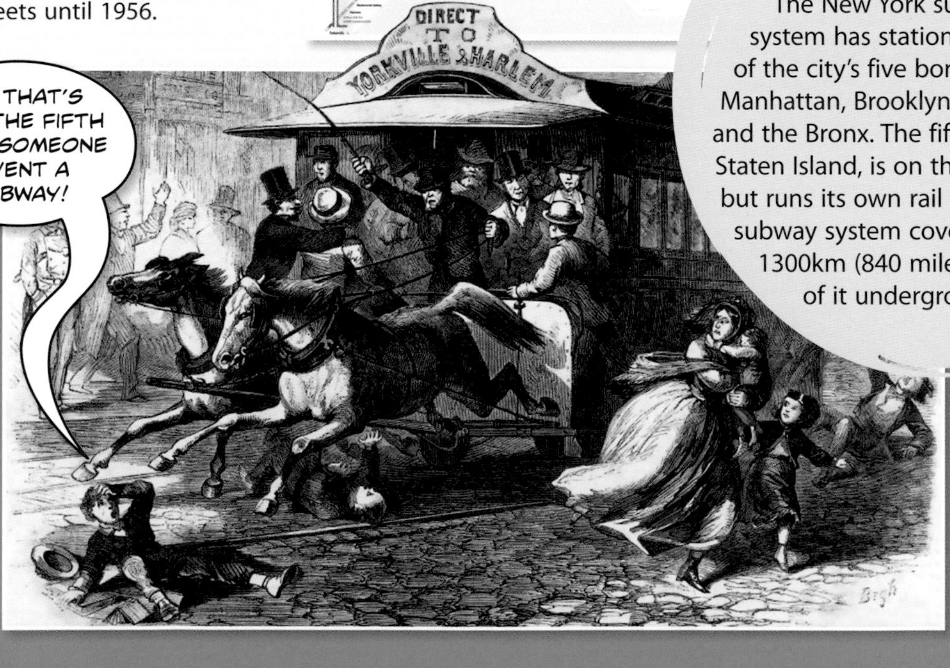

SAVED BY SUBWAYS

GOT MY TICKET

A C E 1 2 3 7 S 4

If trains just barrelled through the city streets you'd think there would be accidents, and you'd be right. In New York City, when steam engines first came on the scene, they travelled along tracks laid on the roads, often crashing into horse-drawn carriages, making people sick from smoke, and drowning out the city with noise. No wonder trains were sent underground.

Rats love the subway!

MY MUSIC IS SO UNDERGROUND

Busker business

Some of the buskers on New York subway stations are part of a program called Music Under New York. The performers are chosen from mass auditions at Grand Central Terminal every Spring.

Not pretty but it works...

Over half the people in New York don't own a car, which is why almost five million passengers ride the subway every day. It may not look pretty – there are rats and rubbish – but the massive system runs 24/7.

WANT MORE?

New York Transit Museum – www.mta.info/mta/museum

ANDY WARHOL

Who would have thought that paintings of soup tins could change the face of modern art? Andy Warhol, that's who. He was the mega-star of New York's Pop Art scene in the 1960s with his paintings and prints of famous brands and famous people. He thought these everyday images were good subjects to explore and experiment with. Millions of people around the world bought his art, and still do, so he must have been right!

ATTENTION SEEKER

From a young age Warhol was into making big money and becoming seriously famous. Painting Campbells soup tins and celebrities like actress Marilyn Monroe made him different from other Pop artists and got him the attention he wanted. He described himself as 'deeply superficial'!

Risky business
Not everyone in New York looked up to Andy Warhol. In 1968 a woman who had worked at his studio shot him and almost killed him!

Warhol painted 32 Campbells soup varieties

Party factory

Warhol's art and film studio was also a factory that mass-produced prints of his work, which is why he called it the Factory! It became party central as well – anyone who was anyone was there, or wanted to be there. The Factory moved locations but was always called the Factory.

Andy Warhol worked here

Funky films

As well as creating prints and paintings, Andy Warhol made movies – weird movies. *Empire* is just a slow-motion shot of New York's Empire State Building at night. The camera doesn't move at all. What's more, the movie is over eight hours long! The most action you see is when the building's exterior floodlights are turned on...

IT'S ALL SILVER

Warhol was mad for silver. His studio, the Factory, was covered with tin foil and silver paint, and had silver balloons floating along the ceilings. At one point Warhol even made his hair silver! That's why the larger-than-life statue of him in Manhattan is shiny chrome.

WANT MORE?

The Andy Warhol Museum – www.warhol.org

SLAMMED!

Big people moving quickly in a small space – that's the action at the West 4th Street amateur basketball court in New York, also called The Cage. It's smaller than regulation size so the fight for the ball is fast and furious. There's no sponsorship and there's no seating – spectators plonk a chair behind one of the baskets or watch from the hectic sidewalk right next to the court. At The Cage the only thing that matters is the game.

Road to remember
In the Bronx area of New York there's a street named Stickball Boulevard, which is also known as Steve Mercado Way, after a local firefighter and stickball player who died in the 9/11 attacks.

Basket-brawl
Many New Yorkers play a tough type of urban basketball known as 'streetball' on small, tight courts where players ignore the sidelines and even the rules!

WHAT GOES UP, MUST COME DOWN...

IT PAYS TO BE A PRO!

The very best streetballers might graduate to become professional basketball players. The top teams in the city are the New York Knickerbockers (better known as the 'Knicks') for men and New York Liberty for women. Both teams play home games at Madison Square Gardens in the heart of Manhattan.

OTHER GAMES IN THE URBAN JUNGLE

Simple and streetsmart

Stickball began as a game that kids could play in the streets with a broom handle and rubber ball. The rules of the game changed from one neighbourhood to another. These days there's an official New York stickball league for children and adults.

It's a hit!

Lots of locals get sweaty using their hands to hit rubber balls against walls. They're playing handball, a sport that was introduced to New York by Irish immigrants more than 100 years ago.

WANT MORE?

Introduction to stickball – www.streetplay.com/stickball/introduction

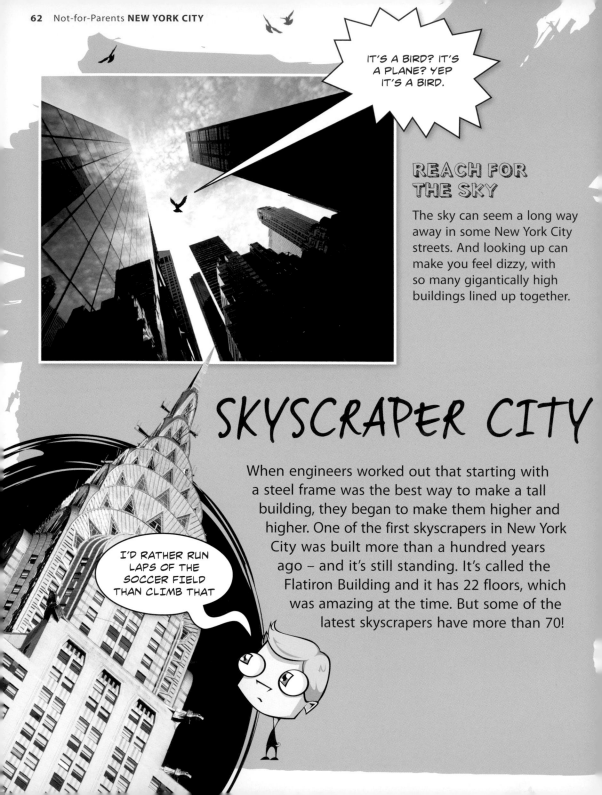

IT'S A BIRD? IT'S A PLANE? YEP IT'S A BIRD.

REACH FOR THE SKY

The sky can seem a long way away in some New York City streets. And looking up can make you feel dizzy, with so many gigantically high buildings lined up together.

SKYSCRAPER CITY

When engineers worked out that starting with a steel frame was the best way to make a tall building, they began to make them higher and higher. One of the first skyscrapers in New York City was built more than a hundred years ago – and it's still standing. It's called the Flatiron Building and it has 22 floors, which was amazing at the time. But some of the latest skyscrapers have more than 70!

I'D RATHER RUN LAPS OF THE SOCCER FIELD THAN CLIMB THAT

SHAPES AND SIZES

The architects who design skyscrapers can make them in loads of different shapes, which is much more fun than lots of square buildings. But they all have to start with a huge hole dug in the ground to make really strong foundations.

One World Trade Center, 105 floors, 541m (1776ft), year 2013

Empire State Building, 102 floors, 381m (1250ft), year 1931

Bank of America Tower, 54 floors, 366m 1200ft, year 2008

Chrysler Building: 77 floors, 320m (1050ft), year 1930

New York Times Building 52 floors, 319m (1046m), year 2007

Sky garden
Just because you live at the top of a really tall building doesn't mean you can't grow your own veggies. And it saves having to go all that way down in the lift to visit the shops.

DAMN WIND TUNNEL

Swirling winds
When lots of tall buildings are close together the wind swoops down off the high walls and swirls around at street level. People who are used to this know to hang onto their hat – or umbrella!

WANT MORE?

New York skyscrapers – www.aviewoncities.com/nyc/skyscrapers.htm

CURTAIN CALL

Musicals on Broadway in New York can run for years. *The Phantom of the Opera* has been running for over 20 years, while *The Lion King* and *Mamma Mia* are both past the ten-year mark. To be 'on Broadway' a theatre must have at least 500 seats. Otherwise it's 'off Broadway'.

Broadway by night
Back when electricity was the hottest new technology, theatres on Broadway had the bright idea of using electric bulbs to add some razzle-dazzle to their signs. Broadway became known as 'The Great White Way'.

Billy Elliot
It was first a film, then a play on London's West End, and from November 2008 it's been on Broadway. Billy Elliot is the story of a young boy growing up in a working-class mining town who wants to be a classical dancer. Four actors alternate as Billy and as the years go on, new Billies come and go!

Broadway is a main road through the city. The theatre district begins at 42nd Street.

I COULD BE A JAZZERCIZE INSTRUCTOR

Lion King

An incredible African spectacle, the stageplay *Lion King* is an adaptation of the Disney film. It began on Broadway in 1997, first at the New Amsterdam Theatre where the huge billboard in the heart of Times Square became famous, and then moving to the Minskoff Theatre in 2006.

Phantom of the Opera

The longest running show on Broadway is *Phantom of the Opera*, the story of a disfigured music composer who haunts the Paris Opera House. The dramatic sets require around 20 scene changes involving 280 candles, more than 225kg (500lb) of dry ice, and a load of smoke and fog machines!

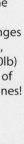

WANT
MORE?

Official website – www.broadway.com

READY OR NOT... HERE WE COME

FROM MARS TO MANHATTAN

New York has been sucked in a few times. There was the hoax about wild animals escaping from Central Park Zoo. There was the rumour of giant alligators in the sewers. And then there was the biggie – the invasion of New York by aliens. It was October 30, 1938 – the day before Halloween – when a radio program broadcast a play adapted from *The War of the Worlds,* a novel about Martians invading earth...

Ugly aliens
During the broadcast, an actor playing a reporter gave a frightened description of an alien: 'The mouth is v-shaped with saliva dripping from its rimless lips that seem to quiver and pulsate...'

Orson Welles

Too good an actor
Before television, radio was the nightly entertainment. Orson Welles was a brilliant actor who knew how to capture an audience's attention. He broadcast *The War of the Worlds* as though it was happening live. No wonder people freaked!

Official confirmation
It didn't help the panic when actors playing government officials 'confirmed' that the United States was under threat from an invading force of Martians and people should run for their lives!

WANT MORE?

TUNNEL VISION

Those who didn't hide under their houses ran from their homes and jumped into their cars to get out of Manhattan. The newly-built tunnel under the Hudson River was quickly jammed with traffic.

FICTION BECOMES FACT

At the start of the program the audience was told it was fictional. So why the panic? Some say that people who didn't actually hear the program were told to panic by people who had only heard part of the program, and when news of the panic hit the real news, the whole thing snowballed!

Have you been abducted by aliens? – www.ehow.com/how_2063368

WHAT LURKS BENEATH

There's an urban legend that alligators breed in New York sewers and regularly turn up in the city's waterways. The story goes that baby 'gators were once brought up from Miami as pets but were flushed down toilets when they got too big, which is how they got into the sewers. So not true. New York rivers are reptile free!

JUST SET ME FREE IN THE SEWERS ALREADY

Close encounters
Back in the 1930s, workers in New York City's sewers wore waders and used shovels when they cleared blockages in the sewerage system.

Far from home
This baby caiman, a South American cousin of the alligator, was found enjoying a swim in a Central Park pond. But he certainly didn't walk there from home.

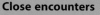

STEAM HEAT

Under New York's streets there is a huge network of pipes that carry steam to office buildings and apartments for heating. If rain drips down onto the pipes, or if any of the old pipes break, clouds of steam rise up through grates and manhole covers. Great way to give passing cars a steam clean.

SEWERGATOR MAN

In the 1930s Mr Teddy May was the go-to man if you needed to know about New York sewers. He'd worked in the sewers for most of his life and was often a witness in court cases because of evidence he'd found underground. So when Teddy told author Robert Daley that he'd seen a whole colony of 'gators, each around 60cm (2ft) long, Daley put it in his book *The World Beneath the City*, and a great urban legend was born!

YEAH I'M REAL. BELIEVE THIS!

WANT MORE?

Steam heating industry – www.coned.com/history/steam

OLD-SCHOOL COOL

One hundred and fifty years ago **F**rederick **A**ugust **O**tto Schwarz came from Germany to New York and started a toy shop. Back then, a china doll was high tech and a wooden toy soldier was every boy's dream. The shop is still going, it's still selling dolls and wooden soldiers, and it's still the place every kid heads to first in New York....

Potter madness

THIS TUNE WILL SLEIGH 'EM!

Keys to fame
FAO Schwarz is famous for its giant
electronic piano keyboard on the floor of its New York
store. They sell a toe-tapping mini version for kids.

FAO FYI

* ✮ The store first opened in 1862.
* ✮ Schwarz wanted it to be more like a playground than shop.
* ✮ His three brothers opened toy stores in other cities.
* ✮ The New York shop has moved seven times.
* ✮ It's America's oldest toy store.

Before its opening in 1986, the current shop was wrapped in red cloth and tied up with a white bow.

Toys and treats

The store's Grand Hall is lit by thousands of computer-controlled coloured lights, and in among all the toys is a classic New York confectionery store called FAO Schweetz.

OF COURSE WE HAVE A LIFE-SIZE ZEBRA!

Making an entrance

Millions of tourists visit the store each year, many stopping to have their photos taken with the living toy soldiers that stand outside the glass doors.

Hello dollies

Within FAO Schwarz there are mini-stores like the design-your-own Muppet store, the Barbie store and the doll factory.

WANT MORE?

The big piano featured in the 1988 movie *Big*. ✮ www.fao.com

NYC INVENTIONS

New York has often been home to the world's tallest buildings. If it weren't for lifts, there would be no point in skyscrapers which is why Elisha Otis is famous. He didn't invent the lift but he did invent the safety brake that stopped a lift from falling even if its cables broke. Thanks to Otis, we can leap to the top of tall buildings in a single bound – and not be afraid of falling. But that's not the only great invention to come out of New York.

New-look Santa
Santa – he of the white beard, large tummy and dashing red outfit – made his first public appearance in the Christmas of 1862, not down a chimney but in the New York magazine *Harper's Weekly*. His look was invented by cartoonist Thomas Nast who got his ideas from the poem *Twas a Night Before Christmas* by New Yorker Clement Moore.

CONVINCING THE CROWDS

Elisha Otis wasn't having much luck selling his idea until he took it to the World Fair in New York in 1853. He wowed the crowds by going up in a lift and having someone cut the cables. The lift industry was born.

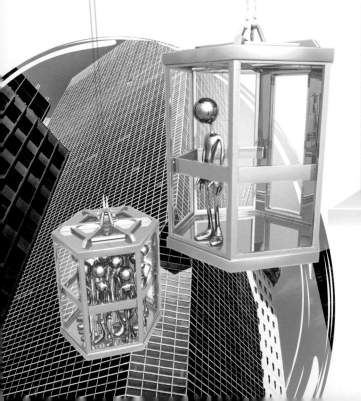

Air Conditioning

Cool air
Willis Haviland Carrier didn't intend to cool the planet when he invented air conditioning. His 'Apparatus for Treating Air' was created to take moisture out of the air so that printing machines could work efficiently. Now we can be cool whenever we want. Thanks heaps Bill!

Lock-it-in

When you next turn a key to unlock a door, think of Linus Yale. He came up with the idea of a flat key with jagged edges that click into place to move a bolt inside a cylinder. You might have used one today.

Toilet Paper

'Personal' paper

The New Yorker who invented packaged toilet paper had his name printed on every sheet! JC Gayetty started selling his flat sheets of moistened paper in 1857. Ten years later toilet paper really caught on when it was put on rolls.

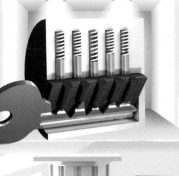
Pin Tumbler Lock

Packaged Jelly

Tuxedo

Easy jelly

Don't ask what it's made of, but thank New Yorker Peter Cooper for instant jelly. He invented powdered gelatin *and* had the bright idea to flavour it and put it in a packet. He also invented the American steam locomotive, but that's another story...

Tuxedo

In the late 1800s men used to wear a coat with 'tails' to formal events. Pierre Lorillard, a rich guy who lived just north of New York in an area called Tuxedo, set a trend by designing a short formal coat. He called it a tuxedo. How did he think of that?

WANT MORE?

Americans once used corncobs as toilet paper – OUCH!

NEW YORK'S BRAVEST AND BEST

In the 1600s when Manhattan was a Dutch colony, wardens called Prowlers, accompanied by citizen volunteers, patrolled the streets at night looking for signs of uncontrolled fire armed only with rattles to raise the alarm and leather buckets made by local shoemakers. An official New York Fire Department has been in operation since 1865.

The ultimate sacrifice
In the rescue mission after planes hit the World Trade Centre towers in Manhattan in 2001, 343 firefighters and paramedics died. Thousands still suffer ill health.

BUCKET TECH

Formal fire brigades were put into service in New York in the 1700s. The first fire engines were two hand-drawn pumpers, brought to America from London. Bucket brigades would bring water to the scene. With the invention of the steam engine, firefighters changed to mechanical pumps.

The stats...
There are over 11,000 fire officers and fire fighters, more than 3000 medical emergency staff and over a thousand civilian employees to look after the fire and medical emergencies of nine million people in the New York area!

CHANGING TRANSPORT

Gone are the days when the department used one type of vehicle depending on what was 'modern' at the time. These days, as well as engines that put water on fires and ladder trucks, there are specialised units to handle hazardous material, medical emergencies and complex rescues and there are fireboats and fire planes.

TOOT TOOT

circa 1915

circa 1922

Today

IF ONLY FIRES WORKED 9-5.

WANT MORE?

New York City Fire Museum – www.nycfiremuseum.org

WALL STREET

Wonder how Wall Street got its name? It was a street that ran along a wall. Clever! Being near the river, warehouses were set up along the street, and soon shops, a city hall and churches followed. In 1792, a group of business men got together to build a place where people could buy and sell stocks in companies, called a stock exchange. Today, Wall Street is the financial hub of America, and the site of the largest stock exchange in the world.

Q&A

Q. *What is a stock?*
It's a piece of a company.

Q. *Why buy a stock?*
If the company does well, the stock is worth more than you paid for it.

Q. *How does the stock exchange make money?*
The stock exchange gets paid every time a stock is bought or sold!

Bull-headed
When a bull fights an enemy, it bucks its horns up into the air, so if the stocks are going up, they call it a 'bull market'. If the market is just showing signs of going up, they'll refer to it as 'bullish'.

Bear this in mind
When a bear attacks, it swipes its paws downwards, so if stocks are going down, they call it a 'bear market'.

BEAR WITH ME!

BUY!
NO, SELL!
NO, BUY!
NO, SELL!
NO...

WALL ST
← 11-21

Before the stock exchange was built people traded stocks underneath a tree on Wall Street.

NERVE CENTRE

The trading room of the New York Stock Exchange, where all the deals are done, is a mad combination of old-school grandeur and high-tech cool. While wireless and cable connections link the trading room to the world, brass bells still signal the start and close of the market each day.

WANT MORE?

The New York Stock Exchange – www.nyse.com/about/history

UN HQ

The United Nations, or UN, is a group of 192 countries that work together to ensure peace, justice and the well-being of all people. Its headquarters are in New York but the land the UN is on is international – it doesn't belong to any one country – so it has its own flag, post office and even its own postage stamps.

SYMBOLS OF PEACE

In June 1954 the United Nations Association of Japan gave UN HQ a bell made out of coins collected from children in 60 different countries. The bell is rung twice a year – on the first day of spring and on September 21 for the opening of the General Assembly, which is also the International Day of Peace.

The UN headquarters building

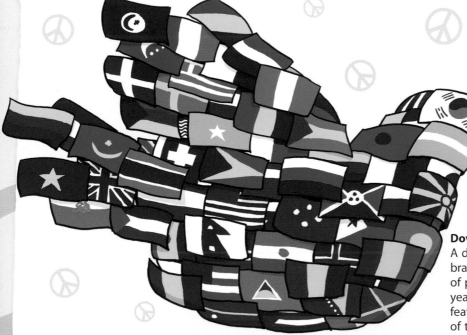

Dove of peace
A dove carrying an olive branch has been a symbol of peace for almost 2000 years. The olive branches feature on the emblem of the UN.

FLAGS OF MEMBERSHIP

UN peacekeeper

Almost every country in the world is a member of the UN. Most are peaceful places, but not all. The UN sends people to help in countries where there is war. The peacekeepers try to keep everyone safe but they can't stay forever. They train local people to take over from them when they leave.

Globe and branches
The emblem of the UN is a world map surrounded by olive branches that represent peace. It is on the UN flag and the stamps sent from the UN HQ post office.

Listen carefully
There are six official languages at the UN: Arabic, Chinese (Mandarin), English, French, Spanish and Russian. Interpreters at UN meetings translate words from one language to another almost as soon as they are spoken. If they make a mistake there could be trouble!

WANT MORE?

The United Nations – www.un.org

I DON'T LIKE PLAYING SECOND FIDDLE TO THIS COSTUME.

Jazz

Jazz was the first American music to influence the rest of the world. It's a style of music that originally came from the African American descendants of slaves in the American south. In the early 1900s, clubs in New York, like the Apollo in Harlem, brought the sound of jazz to the bigger audiences of the Big Apple, and it's been a hit ever since.

Chinese

There's a focus in New York on preserving traditional Chinese styles of music and using age-old instruments like plucked zithers, bamboo flutes and hammered dulcimers. Hammered what? Think of a cross between a xylophone and a harpsichord.

MUSICAL MELTING POT

Take a few million people from all over the world, put them into a tight space with some musical instruments and let the wild rumpus begin. New York is performing arts central. From classically trained artists keeping cultural traditions alive, to musicians who make it up and mix it up, the sounds of the city come from pubs and public halls, fairs and festivals, and the streets and subways.

OK, YOU TRY SMILING AND WHISTLING!

Bolivian dancer

AND THEY SAID PLAYING IN NEW YORK WAS A PIPE DREAM!

St Patrick's Day parade

Arabic

Lots of solo artists, bands and DJs in New York play Arabic music based on a set of musical scales called a *maqam*, which is different to Western scales. The Arabic music scene in New York comes from countries like Egypt, Morocco, Iraq, Israel, Lebanon, Palestine, Syria and Tunisia.

Celtic

The music of Ireland and Scotland, also called Celtic music, is a big part of the city's music scene. There's traditional fiddle music as well as Celtrock – a blend of Celtic and rock. The New York Fire Department even has its own Celtic band.

SOUND CITY

A city that's home to around 800 languages is going to make a lot of different sounds!

WANT MORE?

Musicians who perform in the NYC subway system have to audition for the privilege!

STREET DOGS

Call 'em 'franks', 'weenies', 'wieners', 'red hots' or just plain 'dogs', find a blue and yellow umbrella on a New York street and you've found yourself a hot dog stand. The dogs are stored in warm water, which is why hot dogs are sometimes called 'dirty water dogs'!

CART INFO

The classic New York hot dog stand is a metal cart about 2m (6.5ft) by 1m (3.3ft) in size, selling drinks and other foods as well as dogs. The carts are usually stored in garages overnight and taken to their location the next morning.

What goes around...

Sausages, wieners and frankfurters don't become hot dogs until they're in a wrapping. In New York that wrapping isn't always a standard bun – there are bagel dogs, French fry dogs, corn dogs and bacon dogs!

GLOBAL FEAST

Hot dog stands often also sell pretzels – a bready pastry in the shape of a knot that comes plain, salty or sweet. Pretzels were originally German but are now a common New York street food. The same is true of tamales from Mexico, Indian dosas, waffles from Belgium, Chinese dim sum and Middle Eastern falafel.

CART CULTURE

Running a street cart in New York isn't easy. There are thousands of food carts so there's a lot of competition to get the best position for your cart and to attract the passing crowds. Plus there are big fines for breaking any of the rules, like where carts can be placed, how food is to be displayed and what receipts must be kept.

corn dog

pretzel

hot dog

falafel

The Vendy Awards are an annual competition to find the best street food vendor in the city.

WANT MORE?

The New York Street Food site – www.newyorkstreetfood.com

NOT SO PEACEFUL PEACE

There are heaps of impressive street sculptures in New York City and many of them were designed to be symbols of peace. The city isn't often a peaceful place, but the sculptures represent something that makes people at least think about peace. Some are made up of figures and really tell a story.

A HANDFUL OF HISTORY

★ There are around 300 sculptures in New York's parks and squares.

★ A statue of Joan of Arc, riding a horse and wearing armour ready for battle, stands in Riverside Park near the Hudson River.

★ The city's animal sculptures include a charging bull, eagles, bears, boars and a heap of horses.

Saved sculpture

A big round sculpture, created by Fritz Koenig in 1971 as a symbol of world peace, sits in Battery Park in New York. Called *The Sphere*, it used to be in a plaza in the World Trade Center complex. It was saved out of the rubble after planes hit the World Trade Center twin towers in 2001.

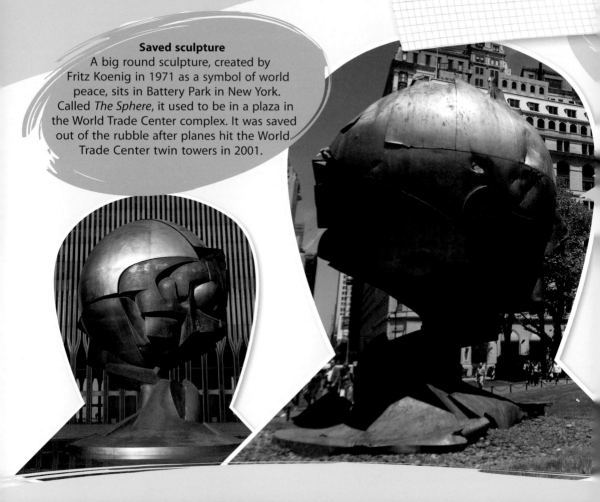

ONE WORLD

The Unisphere is one very large sculpture. It represents Earth, so it needs to be big and it is – the same height as a 12-storey building! And it weighs as much as 60 elephants. It is made of steel and was designed to be a symbol of world peace.

NEW YORK: A GREAT BIG OUTDOOR ART MUSEUM!

Fountain in name only

The Peace Fountain has a lot going on – the angel St Michael has beheaded Satan, a lion and lamb hang out together, there's a giant crab, a sun facing East, a moon facing West, and nine giraffes. The only thing it hasn't got is water!

I'M ON MY FEET 24/7!

Cool cats

This sculpture in New York is one of many cat sculptures in major cities around the world created by the same sculptor, Fernando Brotero.

WANT MORE?

Unisphere ☆ queens.about.com/cs/attractions/p/Unisphere.htm

WELCOME TO WORSHIP

When the twin towers of the World Trade Center in New York were destroyed in a terrorist attack that killed thousands and ruined the lives of many, the city's churches, mosques, synagogues and temples became part of the emergency response services. Faith communities played a huge role in providing practical, emotional and mental support. Religion had never been so important in the Big Apple.

I PRAY MY LIPSTICK SHADE NEVER GETS DISCONTINUED

Buddhist temple
New York's biggest Buddhist temple, with the largest Buddha, is the Mahayana Buddhist Temple. Its Buddha is 5m (16ft) tall. Before becoming a place of worship in 1997, the building was a cinema!

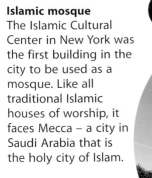

Islamic mosque
The Islamic Cultural Center in New York was the first building in the city to be used as a mosque. Like all traditional Islamic houses of worship, it faces Mecca – a city in Saudi Arabia that is the holy city of Islam.

Jewish synagogue
The oldest Jewish house of worship in continuous use in New York is the Central Synagogue. It was built in the late 1800s, when it was popular for synagogues to have a Moorish style, which is why it has the large copper domes.

DISASTER TRAINING

After the attacks, leaders from different religions and charities got together to create New York Disaster Interfaith Services. They train faith communities in New York on how to handle natural and man-made disasters.

Catholic cathedral
The biggest Catholic cathedral in all of America – is St Patrick's Cathedral. St Patrick's hosted many funerals of police and firemen who died in the attacks on the city in 2001.

WANT MORE?

New York Disaster Interfaith Services – www.nydis.org

LITTLE ITALY

ONIONS MAKE ME CRY

Italy was one of the most overcrowded countries in Europe, so Italians came to New York looking for work. Most were from small villages and had little education but they were hard workers. They found jobs based on physical labour, in factories or on construction sites. They lived close to each other in the part of Manhattan known as 'Little Italy'.

Tough life

The main street of Little Italy, Mulberry Street, has come a long way since 1900 when living in Little Italy wasn't a whole lot of fun. Families had to jam in together in run-down apartments where deadly diseases like tuberculosis spread quickly.

Festivals and food

Every year for over 85 years the sausage has sizzled and the pizza ovens have gone into overdrive in Little Italy during the San Gennaro Festival, a religious parade and feast that raises money for charity.

National colours

Little Italy may be shrinking as Chinatown gets bigger but there's still plenty of Italian colour!

NAME THAT ITALIAN!

MAYBE LADY GAGA CAN BORROW MY ARMOUR SOMETIME

Stefani Joanne Angelina Germanotta – Lady Gaga – is the daughter of an Italian New Yorker. Rudolph Giuliani – New York mayor for seven years – is the grandson of an Italian New Yorker. Giovanni da Verrazzano – the first European to explore New York Harbor – was an Italian.

Giovanni Verrazano

War in the way

The wave of Italian immigrants that hit America from 1880 stopped around 1914. World War I made it too dangerous for civilians to travel by ship.

Rudy Giuliani

Lady Gaga

WANT MORE?

Little Italy – www.littleitalynyc.com

THE ROCK ROCKS!

Rockefeller is a big name in New York and it started with John Davidson – JD. He was determined to make it rich. As a teenager he saved his money and then went into business selling farmyard tools. That didn't make him rich so he sold that business and went into oil refining, buying crude oil pumped out of the ground and refining it for use in engines. Within a few years he was the world's wealthiest man!

If at first you don't succeed...
JD Rockefeller went into the growing business of oil refining but he could see a block to making big money – the cost of transporting the oil. So he forced a good deal with the railway company. Jackpot!

Generous wealth
JD Rockefeller Junior, son of the world's richest man, wasn't interested in making money. He was interested in spending it – on other people. In the Great Depression he created jobs by financing the building of the huge Rockefeller Center, which has given New Yorkers joy ever since. A huge Christmas tree and outdoor ice skating rink are set up there every winter.

SHARING THE WEALTH

The Rockefellers weren't the only family making big bucks in the 19th and early 20th centuries. This period of industrial growth made a few families very, very rich. Fortunately some of these families believed in giving something back to society. Often New York got the benefit of their generosity

Founder

Andrew Carnegie

YOU CAN BANK ON THE MORGANS

Industry

Steel

Legacy

Carnegie Hall concert venue

JP Morgan

Banking

Metropolitan Museum of Art

Cornelius Vanderbilt

Railroads and shipping

Education

WANT MORE?

The Rockefeller Center – www.rockefellercenter.com

TAXI!

Taxi today

You're in a crowded city with hundreds of cars of all shapes, sizes and colours streaming past you. Guess what colour your eyes will notice first? That's why New York taxis, also known as cabs, are yellow. To become a 'cabbie' – one of the drivers of the 13,000 taxis on New York streets – you have to go to taxi school and pass a physical!

River taxi

Hackney carriage

LIGHT SIGNALS

If you want to hail a cab in New York, you first have to know what the lights on top of the car mean.

Colourful history

In the 1800s New York cabbies drove horse-drawn carriages called hackney carriages. In 1907 a businessman, Harry Allen, brought a fleet of petrol-powered cabs over from Europe. They were shiny red and green. He painted them yellow so they would stand out, and the rest is history!

OFF DUTY 6T16 **OFF DUTY**

Medallion number (centre) light is lit = cab available

OFF DUTY 6T16 **OFF DUTY**

Medallion number and side lamps are lit = cab off-duty.

1946 Ford taxi

OFF DUTY 6T16 **OFF DUTY**

No lights are lit = cab already has a fare.

Speed streets

A New York taxi driver, Jacob German, was given the first speeding ticket in America. It was May 20, 1899. He was going just over 19 km/h (12 mph) and he was arrested by an officer on a bicycle!

WANT MORE?

Inside an NYC taxi – www.pbs.org/wnet/taxidreams/panoramas

INDEX

NOT-FOR-PARENTS
NEW YORK
EVERYTHING YOU EVER WANTED TO KNOW

1st Edition
Published August 2011

Conceived by Weldon Owen in partnership with Lonely Planet
Produced by Weldon Owen Pty Ltd
59–61 Victoria Street, McMahons Point
Sydney NSW 2060, Australia

Copyright © 2011 Weldon Owen Pty Ltd

WELDON OWEN PTY LTD

Managing Director Kay Scarlett

Publisher Corinne Roberts

Creative Director Sue Burk

Senior Vice President,
International Sales Stuart Laurence

Sales Manager, North America Ellen Towell

Administration Manager,
International Sales Kristine Ravn

Managing Editor Averil Moffat

Project Editor Lachlan McLaine

Designer Sarah Taylor - Spicy Broccoli Media

Images Manager Trucie Henderson

Production Director Todd Rechner

Production and Prepress Controller Mike Crowton

Published by
Lonely Planet Publications Pty Ltd ABN 36 005 607 983
90 Maribyrnong St, Footscray, Victoria 3011, Australia

ISBN 978-1-74220-497-0

Printed in Singapore

A WELDON OWEN PRODUCTION

Credits and acknowledgments

Key tcl=top center left; tl=top left; tc=top centre; tcr=top center right; tr=top right; cl=centre left; c=center; cr=center right; bcl=bottom center left; bl=bottom left; bc=bottom center; bcr=bottom center right; br=bottom right; bg=background

7tr, 12b, 13tl, t, 17bc, br, 21tr, 28tl, 36cl, 43t, 47tl, 55c, 68tl **Alamy**; 46tl, 55tl **Art Resource**; 17cl, cr, 20tl, 40tr, cr, 40-41b, 41cl, c, cr, 49r, bl, 54cr, 55cr, 57br, **Bridgeman Art Library**; 8b, 12cl, 14bl, 16b, 18tl, 19tl, 20br, 22b, 22-23c, 23tl, bl, 24, 25cl, cr, bl, br, 31tr, 32-33b, 33cl, 35tl, 36-37, 43cl, 45cl, 47cl, 50b, 52b, 55cl, bl, 56b, 58tr, bl, 65br, 67cl, tr, 68r, 71bl, 74bl, 75t, b, 77bg, bl, 80tr, 81tl, 87tr, 88tr, 90bc, 92cr **Corbis**; 59r **Dan DeLuca**; 10br, 20r, 21bl, 28b, 29tr, br, 33t, 36tr, 39tr, 45r, 51c, 52tr, 56tl, 58br, 59b, 60b, 61tl, bl, br, 63bl, br, 64b, 65cl, 68tcr, 70tr, 71cl, r, 74tr, 75tl, 70tl, 80tl, 84bl, br, 89r, br, 91tr, cr, 92tl, 94tcr **Getty Images**; 6cr, br, 7cr, 9tl, br, 11bl, bcl, 12tr, 14c, r, 16tr, 21tc, c, bc, 23cr, 26cr, 27t, cr, b, 35br, 37t, 38bl, 44br, 49cr, 51bl, 53tr, cl, 57tr, 59l, 62t, bc, 63t, 66t, 72tr, 73cr, 78tr, 79cr, bc, 80tc, bc, 81tcl, tc, 83l, cl, bcl, bc, 91tc, c, bc, br, 92tr **iStockphoto.com**; 42b, 43bl, br **Kobal Collection**; 49c **Lego Group**; 20bl, 34l, 36bl, 41tcr **Lonely Planet**; 18c **Picture Desk**; 11br, 21cr, 44tr, c, 47tr, 57l, 62bl, 69t, 79t, 83r, 85tl, 90-91bg, 90l **Photolibrary**; 7cl **Public domain**; 6bl, 7bl, 9tr, 15bg, 17tc, 19tr, 25tr, 26tl, br, 27tr, cl, 30tr, 31cr, 32t, 35br, 38bl, 38-39b, 39tl, 41tl, 44bl, 49t, 51tr, 53tcl, b, 54cr, 60tr, 61tr, 64-65bg, 65tl, 66br, 67cl, 68tc, tr, b, bl, br 69bc, br, 72bl, bc, c, cr, tcr, 73bg, t, cl, 75tr, bl, 76b, cr, 79bl, 80br, 81tr, 82tr, cr, br, 85bl, 86tcl, 89tl, t, cl, 90cr, 92tcr, br, 93, 94tcr **Shutterstock**; 13br **Silverstein Properties**; 8tr, 8-19b, 32tr, 34br, 35tr, 41tc, 49tr, 54tr, 55tc, 56tr, 85br, 86tl, 87t, cl, 88b, 89bcr, 90tr, 9tl, cl, bl **Wikipedia**

All repeated image motifs courtesy of **iStockphoto.com**.

Illustrations

Cover illustrations by Chris Corr

82c, 94tc, tr, bcl, 95tl, tr, bl **Chris Corr**; 22tr, 30-31b, 32bl, bcl, 33r, 54bl, 70c, 74cr, 81b, 82b, 92bl **Geraint Ford/The Art Agency**; 73tl **James McKinnon**; 48b **Michael Saunders**; 78b **Dave Smith/The Art Agency**

Maps and diagrams 17bl, 45bl, 50tr **Peter Bull Art Studio**

All illustrations and maps copyright 2011 Weldon Owen Pty Ltd.

LONELY PLANET OFFICES

Australia Head Office
Locked Bag 1, Footscray, Victoria 3011
Phone 03 8379 8000 Fax 03 8379 8111
Email talk2us@lonelyplanet.com.au

USA
150 Linden St, Oakland, CA 94607
Phone 510 250 6400 Toll free 800 275 8555 Fax 510 893 8572
Email info@lonelyplanet.com

UK
2nd fl, 186 City Rd, London EC1V 2NT
Phone 020 7106 2100 Fax 020 7106 2101
Email go@lonelyplanet.co.uk